The
Waiting Child

Mel Takahara

GARDEN OAK PRESS
RAINBOW, CALIFORNIA

Garden Oak Press
1953 Huffstatler St., Suite A
Rainbow, CA 92028
760 728-2088
gardenoakpress.com
gardenoakpress@gmail.com

First published by Garden Oak Press on May 15, 2019
ISBN-13:   978-1-7323753-4-5
ISBN-10:   1-7323753-4-8

Printed in the United States of America

To

the memory of **Dr. John Unterecker**
my mentor in poetry and life during
a critical period of my development

Barbara, my partner in everything
our children, **Mark** and **Sumie**
my brothers, **Glen** and **Jeffrey**
my mom and source, **Margaret**
our precious granddaughter, **Kaia Margaret**

CONTENTS

The
Waiting Child

Mel Takahara

GARDEN OAK PRESS

MOHAN'S SONG

I dream of sitting under a tree
with you
is it in Vietnam, Honolulu, Escondido, Balboa
Park or Paris?
I cannot tell; it doesn't matter
the leafy shade on grass and dirt will calm our spirits
so we can be still in each other's presence
no mind games
no verbal parrying
or gymnastics
just being
together
I yearn for that
two ships at anchor
berthed together in a harbor at peace.

or maybe we are under a tree in a large garden
that embraces us with beauty and tranquility.
We both see and understand that the beauty around us
flows through us and binds us together
the happy child heart in each
calling to the other in words not yet learned
eagerly telling every secret
the future calls to the past to the future to the now
and we are its echoes

how have we so quickly come to this?
this infinite comfort
or we can simply have mundane talk
to get to know each other
It is good to know what possibilities exist
when we place our oars into the water to begin
the journey under a tree

Tanka are remnants
Ikebana of discourse
multifaceted
fruit of the gem-cutter's craft
blossoms reflected in stone

picking puka shells at Sunset Beach

child man kneeling in coarse warm sand
digging around lava rock through coral detritus
searching for tiny metaphors for life
purple, yellow and brown fragments of shells
that once contained living creatures
now gathered for stringing together into necklaces
to grace tan collars

he embraces the instant of islandness
as though it were some kernel of now
never to be lost

abandoned to the task
bathed by the sound
of waves hissing on sand
while the surfers on the horizon wait on their boards

the old poet picks through shards of memories

trying to make sense
of a stroke I am reeling
my soul is cut loose
from its mooring once again
I am a flung stone hurtling

the infant mouths the unspoken
touch retreats from all surfaces
rhythmless
unpaced
unmasked finally
face to face
this is a beginning
this is the end
tail biting the head
I am the serpent

like a mosaic
fragments of life now cohere
into a clear message
from some dimly remembered
kingdom which is my true north

this valley

sitting in my sunlit zen garden
a stone's throw from the old creek
I google Luiseno and am immersed
in indigenous history

beyond the bamboo fence

Adamlike he does not know his nakedness
kneeling among the oaks
by the stone spirit guarding the stream
his bow touching the ground

in garden shadows are paths
of hunters and gatherers
struck, my singing bowl resounds

beyond the range of sound
in great stillness
all are together in friendship
embraced warmly in silent harmony
this valley has long been a gathering place

the creek is its living heart
connected to the sea
and to the sky
and the beyond where in nakedness

we are all hunters and gatherers

I am led to profound gratitude
that the Luiseno had no Trail of Tears to march
they were not hunted down
to be exterminated

I think of myself
reflected on the surface
lanterns for the dead
are floating all around me
the taiko can still be heard

their blood did not stain
creek waters flowing past homesteads
their blood did not soak
into earth that would soon produce
green and purple Muscat grapes

we are all hunters and gatherers

their cries did not fly like
bird cries into the wild wind
echoless shriek in time
punctuated by gunshot

I realize that this land is innocent
my heart is lightened

we are all hunters and gatherers

this is home

my mom at ninety
talks of a brother who drowned
while still a toddler
she does not know where he lies
my unknown unnamed uncle

Richard Bartley

While searching through black and white
aerial photos of our city at the history center
I was assisted by a volunteer in the archives
a kind man with a deep love for the hidden valley,
he joined my search eagerly and soon produced
a view from 1968 which clearly showed the
original Escondido creek like a smudgy worm
touching the end of a double white line
like the no-crossing lines on a 2 lane highway
the dark smudgy worm was the creek
which had been prone to flooding in heavy rains
The white lines touching the worm
were the sides of the half-completed flood
control channel
the black band between the white lines
was the neatly contained stream of
channelized creekwater
rendered innocuous in its controlled, elegantly simplified form
a line of calligraphy on the land like a brand on hide

We talked of then and now and before then.
He seemed to live there on that side, beyond the then.
He reached out with his arms to show how
after school on rainy days,
he would grab his prized home-made raft
to then go running to the flooded crossing at Fig
where he waded in with the raft for a ride
and he was this perfectly lovable kid having the time of his life.
That was 5 years ago.
I reached out for him recently and was told he was gone,

passed 3 years ago at 80
but still in my mind's heart he rides the swollen creek
on that homemade raft, still 15,
with eternal grin and pounding heart
himself becoming the brown water
laughingly flowing swiftly to the sea
Now, when we walk along the creek at dusk
my wife counts the remaining baby mallards
of this season's hatchlings scattered in the
shallow stream below

around their mother at the bottom of the
concrete channel
with high sloped sides on each cemented bank

and when we cross the intersection of Fig,
I ache and rejoice.
The monumental simple lines and monotone of
concrete giving comfort
in the fading bastard amber light.

Gone. the favorite tree.
House too. Foundation melted.
All consumed in flame
Pyrocumulus demon
coats everything in thick ash.

clung to thoughts of death
shipwrecked my soul seeks relief
from unceasing pain
of the loss of the beloved
stars circle the dark center

sound of sound fades
it is no longer music
or voice of the beloved
taste of taste vanishes
without trace of after taste
sight of sight shrinks
into the darkness
whispering of shades
lisped to death
slithering out of the embracing light
flayed.

the soot blackened stream
that reflected fiery tongues
now flows clear again
white and pink camellias
handpicked, strewn, floating downstream.

the bicycle pedal
had nothing to do
with me until I sat
at the table next to it
and stared at it wondering
whose foot had last pushed it
to the bottom
of the ferris wheel circle
as we glide over the ground
I see the bare foot planted
on the beat up pedal
and feel a heart beating
in flight response
pursued by the past
a smaller foot pristine
hurtling into now
to the sounds of a night fair.

this hurt is not me
it occupies just a part
of a whole being
whose chambers once resounded
with music and sounds of life

Lorca Fantasy

Drawn by your eyes
I entered the room and bravely chose
to sit next to you
eighty-seven years ago
in six years you would be captured
and executed by the Nationalists

our hands met behind us
shyly affirming
wordlessly

on that other moonlit night
the car pulled to the side of the country road
and you were pulled from the back seat

how I would pull you back into safety
but our hands no longer reach each other

you stand before the wall
in darkness
the other side glows white in the moonlight
you yearn for the fragrance of flowers in the chill
night air

he comes from behind
a venomous spider
you are fair prey

you see only the colorful dancers arriving
for the celebration

I've come to this place
of healing to cover pain
with blankets of warmth
now and after now until
grasses bow low with their seed

Hermana mia

for Teresa Gonzales Lee

she has gone ahead but her spirit beckons
from the meditative anteroom
where I slip into and out of dream

ever the teacher, she whispers common truths in
my ear
and delights the very core of my being
with the sudden elation of Lorca's bugs
their secrets scrubbed of all fear
sung like childsong for all to hear where she is
now,

the memory of heart expanded,
of joy exceeding all logic and circumstance
is utterly supplanted, fully informed by eternal
truth

eternal love

now her poetic impulse is perfectly fulfilled
in the garden
adios hermana mia

*the two voices sing
old and new in unison
surrounding the now
embracing me in their love
I know I'm the song being sung*

14

The boy from Idlib

like a fish too long
out of water
he gasped
reduced to bare essentials
pleading for a clean puff
of time
his child eyes uncomprehending
He was plucked from ocean love of family
before morning prayer
and left stranded on this bleak shore

He musters his whole being to take each frothy breath
deliberately living
pouring himself into the act
like deftly bareback mounting
the waiting pure black Arabian steed
who instantly recognizing his master
prances and wheels
foaming at the nostrils
He rides the night until evening prayer

when I think Life sucks
in the middle of the day
sometimes your image
says, "nut up, and just do it!"
there is no other option

15

To a Lady Tourist

            visiting the paradise of Hawaii
in 1938, staying at The Royal Hawaiian Hotel
            the "pink palace" on Waikiki Beach
among the likes of Ava Gardner and her many
            leading men and husbands
you may not have noticed
            that a floral bouquet delivered to your room
was missing a blossom
            it was my dad who, on the elevator,
plucked that single bloom
            from the abundance of beauty
which he carried to your door in his bellman's
            uniform, gratefully accepting the tip
he did it for the lovely assistant to the Pastry Chef
            who demurely accepted the token of love on her break

thus began the taffeta dream of weekly dances in the
            downtown hotel ballrooms
and courting on Waikiki beach sand. The future was
            ordained as such futures always are.
He has long since gone the way of all flesh
            But, seventy years later, mom still remembers that
flower.
            I just wanted to thank you.

yet on ancient winds
I'm carried into the now
bearing hope of life
unending filled with a love
that forgives every error

Sleep Children

(for Orlando)

In response to the painting by Patrick N. Brown

In the liturgy of dreams
there is confession
there is time for wailing
for screaming and begging
for waiting these final seconds

lifting the consecrated host
sacrament of touch
bridging the eternal gap

exorcism of the abomination of self
in the ecstasy of being

If we had only known by what means
echoing. echoed.
all feel the impulse to tiptoe
into the vast incompleteness

somewhere a mother licks the afterbirth.

This is the aftermath. The prequel.
Purgatorial staging area.
Green room of the apocalypse
eternal synapse.

We are all tissue samples
there is no smell here. It is antiseptic.
It is a sinkhole of incalculable dimensions.
a sudden collapse of all fragility
into shards
a talus slope of ankle bones.

halleluia, halleluia.

Sleep children
dream they have existed
wholly accepted.

Ferlinghetti's Visit

for Lawrence Ferlinghetti on his 98th birthday

Young Lorenzo stepped out
of the rented convertible
like out of a painting by Raphael
into Makaha sunlight
his golden hair glowing.
Great men have beautiful sons
and are solicitous dads.
Sometime during the visit
I managed to show the great poet
my elaborate assemblage poem
which I laid out on the floor for him
He called it "esoteric"
I recognize now it was
a product of undiagnosed mania
Then we took a ride
he drove as I directed into the valley
and he caught sight of the two condo towers
sprouting from the hillside,
valley air exploded as he shouted
"Those Fuckers!!!"
I know who he means
it began with annexation

*as a touch of frost
sometimes kisses persimmons
and leaves them sweeter
be transformed by the winter
and release your own sugar*

Manifest Destiny

these savage hands can't
grasp the wisps of aurora
emanating from my heart
like patchouli
subliminal grief
sweetness of words
containing me
shuddering waves
fibrillating through life
mourning the broken
in the stillness after

mortal breath
disguised as God
commissioned manifest destiny

unleashing dark legions
to the ends of the earth
trailing tears
of First Peoples
counting all as winning and redeeming
as profit
gathering all in a heaping pile on green casino felt
mea culpa, mea maxima culpa

as sea grasses sway
in undulating currents
on the ocean floor
the tide moves in slowly
under the radiant full moon

Born into these ears and heart
We are called to acknowledge
the crumbling step and the abyss
the hurtling pull of the fall
we are created to witness
the reality of evil
registrars of death
the ragged edge of worth
untouchable tenders of funeral pyres
low caste beings
we sing the dirge and alert the universe
to the curse

children play in fields
seasons come and seasons go
delusions remain
like tattered baby blankets
that no longer give comfort

Mohan's Song

Plovers honor the deep
their scattering dance
in the foam
wake of waves
taste and smell of sea
like blood we embrace
a skittering bliss.

yearning to be me
I rummage through the wreckage
of a family home
looking for familiar things
each thing is a face

splayed wings thump to copper
rays glittery my eyelids
flutter my vision wavers
miraging in the shimmering
desolation of my stuttering lust

not knowing to what
I am pulled by the currents
of these five faces
into the swirling maelstrom
of delusional comfort
weeping mangoes cling
to Irises in sunlight
burst of taste and hue
yet the smell of blood pervades
youth is a dreamed garden

brown-skin boy inside
the aging intellectual
searches the landscape
for signs of divine caring
how can the father not weep?

the found sandal triggered electric shame
he could not look at it without
bottomless longing
for the being who once stood
staring into his soul
unsung songs echoing between them

fresh shame renews comfort
newly exposed we pull more covers
to find the warm center
in a dream state we fling them all off
to be embraced

It's all Brahms.

clear, O desert sky
all clutter from my spirit
simplify my heart
give order to my strata
teach me to be forgiving

I turn the page
and look for that lost moment
that roomful of AmeriCorps members
posing for a picture
their powerful energy
and brilliant shirts perfect
in the viewfinder
irretrievable moment
lost in the ether
their beauty flung
to the future

embankment of clouds
imaginary landscape
glimpse of tomorrow
shifting shapes reveal secrets
all vanishing into now

coming to a place of safety
expecting reconciliation
I find light focusing on my darkness
like winds on the mountain range
flushing clouds of pollen from clenched branches
there is song in the air
not whispered
but shouted
alleluias exhaled
I am mountain serpent
and fecund forest
glowing
in the taxonomy of *aumakuas*
I do not yet exist

Did he feel owned
before he took that final breath?

the brothers bore the weight of perfection easily
they were born to it. Clearly they were Ali'i.
they owned everything in sight.
they owned me instantly. Yet, I had no fear
even when one pulled out a dull black handgun
and began firing out the car window
into the dark valley air
as we sped on Auyong Homestead Road

from this crucible
pour forth essence of relief
fragrance of newness
enticing all my senses
with fresh possibilities

like a child finally discovering
his biological dad
after being lost for so long
the prodigal son
has the void in his soul filled

I am transparent
in the sight of the beloved
he sees every flaw
yet he loves and accepts me
an infant on his strong chest

greatness did once befriend me
in the person of a teacher
who walked with giants
yet saw my soul
and recognized the budding shape
of a poet
now that I am here
and you are there,
Jack, I know you will be delighted to know
that I am still budding
even after a stroke
in those raw points of healing,
nubs of new life emerge
spontaneously to reveal my promiscuous heart
in wild whirling dances tracing my delusions
I know you understand and I sorely need to have
this conversation with you
together we could get to the very source of poems
at the convergence of doctrines
In night sky trailing
to the furthest end of the felt arc
till we are left numb and dumb as our sensory
organs fail
like your faulty heart did on that sterile operating
table
your eyes frantic and comprehending
as you joined the circle of Khoros dancers
beginning to sway to the music
in final celebration.

in this great shadow
there are bird sounds arising
from a thousand nests
each bird heart sings a true song
cacophony of true songs

Mililani

The bright path plunges
into the gulch before emerging
unto manicured greens
where rows of pineapple plants
once crowned with iconic fruit
are now replaced with granite markers
planted neatly in the turf
some accented with floral offerings
festive in sunlight
left by the bereft
the tree marks the place
where decades later
we find our roots and shade

in verdant valleys
kids still look for mountain shrimp
in streams under stones
worn smooth over the ages
by clear cool rushing water

A bias to wellbeing

The unfolding of a Monarch's wings
sings a song of wellbeing
a just rightness that perfectly fits
the chrysalis and turns into glory
whose brightness has been calling
all along

we bend to the weight of the impacts
swaying inner surfaces
stretched to aching
then relaxing to completeness
instantium stationary dusk
obsidian humming
dark dancing beings
everywhere twirling
like beasts devouring vacancies
leaving only fullness
settling into complete foundness

in my vivid shadow world
we pulse to the weight
of the impacts

now kindness reaches
into the hidden pockets
of our hurting souls
to get to the nub of pain
like giving one a backrub

O tiny one!

joy anticipated is baby powder sweet
impossibly little toes
to kiss five at a time
a miraculous possibility
yet unnamed
will blossom into our beloved
leaving indelible growth marks
on our hearts
to expand our lives beyond all imagining
as you take your divine place in our lives
you bless us all

*O bud of my heart
unfold into morning air
revealing beauty
give of yourself willingly
to fill empty eyes with joy*

Sing Bell

sing brass
resonate with
left chambered yearning
touch balls of feet
kiss toes
tingling with anticipation
of the song
full throated proclamation
of the heart's layered bowl
ringing
stretched thin
into undulating filament
unwittingly fine
winding through halls of stone
at breathless elevations
grown lightheaded from the lack
of reassurance
we are left floating
in silence

on this sweet journey
may you discover healing
and come to the bay
see the glistening ocean
now beckoning through the trees

at an impressionable age

I now go to sleep with stuffed animals
a monkey whose face makes me smile
and a little black bear who fits perfectly in my hand
we got him in Tennessee after a day
of watching a mama bear with her three cubs
frolicking in the woods of Smokey Mountain
National Park
that was before my stroke
I can still hear the dulcimer playing on the porch
this was Cherokee land
the trailhead
for the trail of tears
green gorges and high valleys are
at a distance
the blue ridge
scalloped landscape receding to the past
dissolving into sky
meadows and ancestral homesteads nestled into
natural confluences of family convenience and comfort
hearths and shelter
rock and water, bark and earth
pleasure centers well-worn
laughter and weeping
woven into the land
overflowing like a leather fringe
on dreamless nights, I hold fast to that little black bear

listen to the muse
she has whispered a secret
and revealed the way
for wounded loved ones to go
into a place of healing

eggs

we're told not to put all our eggs into one basket
which doesn't seem efficient

why carry several baskets
when they can easily fit into just one
what could possibly happen?

well, I suppose the basket could fall
and be run over by a steam roller
or it could fall into a vat of acid

or on a trip to the Pali lookout on Oahu
I could be overtaken by an uncontrollable
impulse to fling it into the upwelling wind
so that it flies tumbling against the backdrop
of green cliffs with eggs falling out in all directions
hurtling through tradewinds
to their tropical end

or I could suddenly discover that
the half dozen eggs in my basket
had become shattered mirrors
No, we should not put all our eggs into one basket

Not being one to tempt fate
I always keep my eggs separate.

seed of healthy joy
be planted deep within me
bud of healthy joy
blossom in my mind and heart
and fill me with contentment

"I love you guys!"
shouted from a distant point
encapsulates the cry of a soul
who sometimes appears
as a skipping shadow
at the periphery
of perceived reality

yellow Hau blossoms
dot the verdant banks
of remembered days
and joy still turns to passion
by evening then fades away

my frail hand reaches to ring for help
but no one responds
because this place is filled with refugees
who each have enough to deal with
enormous exertion to reach

Sumerian Rhapsody

emerging from the babbling
between rivers
language itself comes into being
even the might of a king
cannot prevent reality
from spelling out the death
of a beloved son
inscribed in wedges on clay
would not all of civilization
be best unwound till all surfaces
are no longer blemished
with truths too difficult to bear
the father's wailing
echoes through stone corridors

dancers fill the eye
with a stately symmetry
the procession moves
into unexplored spaces
to challenge the emptiness

Three Coatimundi in a pepper tree

have no smartphones
they do not stand around on sidewalks staring at screens
nor do they suffer
from election regret, remorse, regurgitation
impenitent, they follow each other
around the rock formation
like pilgrims
ring-tailed , feigning innocence
in guilt-laden creation
perpetually seeking
an exit from catastrophe
held back by rings that bind them to the past
and present
I have dreamt of their other existences
as prime ministers, faith leaders and heads of state
could they choose
would they prefer
the sublime security of knowing
that this branch is just an arm's length from that branch

Azalea dream
surrounds the heart with beauty
at the end of sleep
a profusion of blossoms
to adorn the waking soul

waiting for Pinkerton

taller than the garden Cypress
even bootless he stoops to enter
through shoji doors
his bare feet
alabaster on tatami mats
beautiful American Naval feet,
which have felt wood plank decks
awash with seawater
fair-haired young officer
used to having his way
dense as a black hole
his embrace was real as the child she bears
in his absence she continually conjures his presence
he is a delusion hidden in garden shadows
in this shrine to his kami
a shadow world slipping away sideways
as she counts down the days
this reality is out of his mind
she has vanished, erased like youthful error
this will not end well for Butterfly.

in the dark harbor
waits the freighter ship laden
with goods to transform
barren lives with new fullness
seeds on night winds will take

We are all lost dots
seeking another plane
recalling a more perfect time
yearning to reconnect
lost but not forgotten
still ultra-fine
deliberately placed
with fine-motor precision
permanent yet floating in the ether
our lostness defines us
more than the abstract pattern
of our congregate shape,
a murmuration of starlings,
an impulse captured between AA step readings
like in constellations, each star fixed for eternity
precisely where they were intuitively placed
in a universe now lost
yet still in an act of pure love
some quantum duplicate
potential reality might someday
become disentangled and suddenly materialize
as a found notebook

by naming a thing
we can put distance between
us and this demon
this destroyer of my peace
this shatterer of the calm

The descent into madness

was not gradual
but like an elevator plunge
from celestial penthouse to basement
where everything was severed
from meaning and value
then the pain sets in
spreading like dark blood
after the deed
surrounding
radiating from that point
obliterating hope
I yearn for a gun
my wife quietly takes our credit card
from my wallet
now I'm on Zoloft
I still dream of angels

the force of the wave
propels us to the sandy shore
we jumped off the rock
into the blue-green torrent
over and over again

38

EMBRACE OF

THE LIVING GOD

Cast from the garden
they could not hear the father weeping
his heart bereft of the beloved
this new emptiness reminiscent of
the void before creation
but it hurts
the weeping becomes groaning
that fills the universe

*sleeping cat hops off
the morning bed my feet slide
into warmth he left
when I hop out of this life
will I leave such a warm spot?*

the believer dreams of a creator
who cannot truly suffer loss
for whom all change is regenerative

the dreamer clings to the blood-stained feet
of the beloved
whose journey to hell traced
irretrievable loss
eternal powerlessness
permanently sealed tombs to which
the author of permanence has no key

i do not praise a God of lost things
loss is an illusion

looking at the moon
I yearn to see my best self
then I see the sun
reflected back to my life
and the light is forgiveness

Ray

Ray has no shelter tonight
other than his jackets and caps
and a makeshift campsite
in the coastal sage scrub

The final winter storm is gone now
but the night air is still damp
and cold
Perhaps he will dream
of younger sunlit days
in Solana Beach
and frequent family trips
that bound them together
until death unbound them
releasing him to the cold
He recalls with pride ringing
a bell for The Salvation Army
at Christmas
sometimes seven hours daily
for a month for several years
"No rain tonight, thank God."
Warm memories and the absence of rain
are shelter
embracing him with the smell of sage

he dreams of nights at the winter shelter
after days of walking from agency to agency
standing in line at drizzly dusk to be breathalyzed
to get in out of the cold if there is an open cot,
hot supper prepared and served by volunteers
from local churches and community groups
casseroles and stews mainly
talk with a case manager after supper and watch
some tv
then bed down in an army cot with a real pillow and
a comforter
cots stretched from wall to wall as lights dim
it is dry and warm
this is home for the night

the handsome gymnast somehow lost his legs
both amputated
and he has a diagnosis of AIDS
other shelter residents instinctively seek to shield him
from the unshieldable
as he scoots across the floor
intrepid young man with a wholeness that belies his form
his lover once kissed his feet

the couple hooked on heroin and methadone
have carried their daughter's heavy ashes
from car to motel to shelter
she had died in a car accident
and they fell out of their lives
into the broken place
mother lovingly embraces her daughter
she is holding a cardboard box

loyal mother and son
he was bent by a bi-polar father
she was overwhelmed by life
they came to lean on each other
and learned to live on the edges
he looks with yearning at older men
who could have been a normal dad
he would give himself to them
he yearns to go camping
the bright college-age daughter,
loyal and resourceful
was no match for the system
that allowed her mother
to fall out of housing and into the streets
she would not abandon her to dementia
but sought her out and found her
holding onto her in the wind
guiding her into the open doors of shelters
both slept on the floor
within touching distance for reassurance
daughter's heart numb

like the newborn child
on the father's chest
held gently by strong hands
cradled in his embrace
knowing perfect oneness
beloved you are bound for good

beloved I give you
the blessing of my release
with love sufficient
to fill universes
to embrace where 'ere you go

The Virgin kissed the Christ

how could a young mother resist?
those tiny feet!

how could the judged woman resist?
those dirty calloused feet?

in vestments
with a silver vessel of blessed water
the pope washes and kisses the feet
of the poor

how could I resist the feet
of the beloved?
I've been washed with tears and perfume.

sunlit chrysalis
contains a new butterfly
to dot the blue sky
with fluttering orange wings
on silent valley breezes

the beloved was a little boy

the beloved's mother
will always remember
how as a little boy,
he comforted her
with little boy arms
and kind words
of reassurance
that everything
will be okay

such a little embrace
contained infinite
love eternal

brighten the embrace
stick that tight circle of light
into the center
of expanding darkness
at the ending of Act Two

46

Embrace of the Living God

head of the beloved
rests on the breast
of the master's
mortal form

a convenient crook of arm
familiar embrace
effortlessly uncalculated
eternally shaped

mere hours before the fullness of time
is realized in agony

love will not remain
contained

beloved creation is
the poem I gave
for this embrace

abide in me
and i will mend
broken nature

to perfect eternity
with original love
unsealed

*distant sound of surf
becomes a single white line
drawn on the darkness
everything is possible
when it's taken breath to breath*

47

Air China

A young father emerges from the tunnel
walks to his waiting family
and picks up his son.

The boy, suddenly embraced,
stiffens his back
and looks away

As he rides above the others
in his father's arms.

the restored Adam
stands before me in silence
I can hear my breath
as I gaze at his manhood
and his cold size thirteen feet

One cannot avoid eternity forever

There is eventually
a passage from here
from the familiar
from love of family
to there beyond
time and space
deep into God's heart
where we awaken to
love that embraces.

It seems a simple
and self-evident thing
to move from love to love.

tanka are remnants
ikebana of discourse
multi-faceted
fruit of the gem-cutter's craft
blossoms reflected in stone

The impermanence of things

Sometimes the bottoms of things
fall away
like the bottom of a box holding
a precious gift

And we can fall with it
into a broken place.

Or we can fling our goblets
into the stone fireplace
to commemorate the precious moment
of our friendship.

Here is the gift!
unscathed.

When all else has burned away
love shall be merely burnished.

tsunami warning
we kids didn't know better
rushed to the shore
to watch the water recede
then went home disappointed

The creative urge is evidence
of our paternity.

Flame ignited
in the beginning
still glows in each,

Revealing form
in tangled fancy
and flow in flux

pointing to order
announcing presence.

How vast the immensity
of the grasp
embracing all conception.

we were two young guys
on our backs staring at stars
to the sound of surf
I shared my expansive dreams
and you said I scared you

there is a connectedness in reality
that eventually reveals the shape of the imperceptible
suffused with light from votive candles and a great rose window
the barefoot penitent seeks the beloved in the
great stone yearning of a cathedral
he instinctively shouted for help when he couldn't touch bottom
and the haole lifeguard had rescued him
carrying the brown boy to the beach
where he lay on the warm sand, eyes closed,
debating
whether he had really needed rescuing
still feeling the strong arms holding him
he would dream for years of being held
does being rescued count if you don't need to be rescued?

in Waikiki surf
stunned by the long board, he bleeds
on another shore
granddaughter is struck and bleeds
in the same ocean of time

a dream of Paris

a point on the island in the middle of the river
is the center from which all distances are measured
it is a gesture towards divine order that falls short

not so the Spires and gargoyles ascending
stone becomes cloud becomes light becomes
eternity in the dark cathedral,
twilight ignites stained glass window roses
their immensity, expanding beyond walls and buttresses,
unfolding grace.

racks of votive candles flicker
tiny flames stained red and blue by glass
their glow rising in the darkness
subsumed by the light filtering down
from the windows
the kneeling faithful are embraced by stained light

in a nearby garden of loss, Chopin and Morrison, eternal grave
neighbors
find some sublime reconciliation of aesthetics amidst marble
and granite
bulky placeholders for the lost
painstaking clues left of vibrant lives lived
we seek the living among the dead

a block away, the boy with a fresh baguette in arm
rollerskates down the sidewalk
his little white dog running ahead, on a leash,
going home
he yearns for a cathedral of beaches
where there is no loss
only continual finding for a boy and his dog

San Felipe
for Barbara

It is midnight on the beach
of the Sea of Cortez;
silvery white fish break surface and glide
through hot night air
to plash back into the black sea.

And far above the Earth, a meteor
breaks the surface of the atmosphere,
Gliding through night air, igniting:
white, yellow, red, green.

Like mirrored events.
Bright creature straining upward.
Divine flame descending.

Like brackets in time
holding infinity
and we are embraced by them

*the moon reflected on
Pacific horizon
source of my heart's tide
will rise and fall forever
beckoning to my brown soul*

pieta

like duties after a great feast
the task of gathering his body
was attended to by his mother
his cold empty form overflowing her arms
limbs trailing like grief, his gaping side
an image of her own pierced heart

embracing him
she groans.

birdlike memories
long hidden in the shadows
shivering in fear
are released to the new air
revealing themselves at last

Watching daddy die

I felt the release of
    the burst seam
    the snapped rein like a rifle shot aimed at distant
    hills.

The child
bearer of sins
is cast into the arms
of those herded into
the grim dark
hold.

And mountains float in space
while the held child
is comforted.

Wounds have clotting times
ranging from a few seconds
to infinity.

you were my lover
in another perfect life
I have not yet mourned
your death on that sad island
some losses remain untold

Sometimes love

for Barbara

Sometimes love
is doing the dishes and the laundry

watering the plants
gathering oneself from scattered desires
and wishes

focusing strength
on simple necessities

rising to the occasion
as wife and mom

in gesture prayers
the paraclete presence
practiced

sometimes conscious
sometimes not
of the larger context

of the one who subsumes our small wills
and will nots with grace
that flows from infinite love

*you've plucked chords in me
to forgotten songs long-stilled
to songs unwritten
whose meanings are in the wind
whose tunes live in our bodies*

My son's cat

It's been nearly a month
and we still ring the bell at mealtime
still set the bowl out
still look under beds, in the garage, down alleys
still wait for a scratching on the door

we grill his favorite meat
and sit calmly discussing the day
hoping to suddenly feel him brush lightly
against our legs, circling the table

and we think secretly of our own leaving
of those we watched go
of those who went unseen

of their passions and hatreds
our gifts and frailties
deeds and misdeeds
hopes and fears
gains and losses

all neat columns we cling to
surrounded by unseen columns
that threaten to break apart
releasing us from all meaning

how comforting it was to feel
him on my lap
purring

does my pure love count
for currency in this game?
have I no credit
to affect the final score
am I now irrelevant?

beloved my startled heart is humming
i am a shivering bird
hiding from large creatures

i know only that i seek your embrace
my source and destination

i want to pull your comfort about me
your strong hands holding
the child that i am
when did my being
become your being?
when did we become
confused with each other?

we must discover
why the universe has sent
this humble servant
into your earthly service
undoubtedly to do good

All futures are before you

Love, all has been forgiven
the doors that were held closed against the wild man
have been unlocked and left ajar

you can breathe freely now
that time is done
those lessons learned

Let your eyes adjust to the light
expand your heart
relax into the comfort of my embrace
I am with you
all futures are yet before you

every time I see you
you just take my breath away
your mortal presence
defies mere reality
and I am delusional

beloved I pour myself out for you
my blood and life
spilled for you

every blessing in me
is meant for pouring into you

to fill your life with fullness
to complete my joy knowing that I fulfill your life
I am vine to your branch

color of wood ash
like the woodpile she came from
feral Bengal cat
who comes when I call her name
has learned how to call my name

little girl tabernacle

the little girl held by her daddy
suddenly knows things no language
can describe nor image depict

in this moment she contains
the very heart of God
his love filling the universe

the holy flame burns away
all traces of the absence

ocean waves wash clean
the memory of sin

torrent of wind swirls
in celebration of union

The Father too had groaned
for the fullness of time
to fill this emptiness

all is unspoken
the melody goes unheard
but ancient meanings
bind the hapless ones who stand
in totally different nows

O vigilance,
where shall I find secure rest?

in the father's arms.

O soul wandering
outside the gate,
how will I enter the sanctuary?

o sleepless night
how do I escape this endless
expanse of wakeful landscape?

where can I find peace?

in the father's arms.
in the father's arms.
the father's arms.
be held.
be held.

*in you I have found
someone I thought I had lost
I keep finding you
in unexpected places
in unsuspecting people*

63

a cloud of witnesses has watched raptly
the cosmic processional dance to the throne
led by the paschal lamb spirit king

in hilly desert villages
on the seashore
in the mountain city of the temple
in vineyards and groves
as loving son
radical teller of truth
prophet and worker of miracles
master, servant and friend
betrayed and condemned

crucified
buried in stone
bearing the sins of the world

resurrected in glory
yet faithful to look after his flock

ascended and exalted on the throne
the anointed one who forever embraces the world
with the father's arms
like a mother hen

He remembers warm beach sand between his toes

we were just young colts
playing 6th grade tricks
then surprised by peace
in the deep warm silences
of each others' acceptance

Suddenly found, I
quicken to his presence,
transparent
in his brightness, called
as one blameless,
my shielding hands fallen away.

Held,
I am a child waking
to the sanctuary of his embrace.

Natatorium
blue-green sunlit memory
beachside concrete pool
filled with Waikiki water
and the laughter of brown kids

unspeakably sad
these willow branches touching
the water surface
are ghosts yearning to be felt
such are life's missed connections

THE WAITING CHILD

Rising out of water

1.
not graciously
but in a sudden
gushing bleeder
spraying the sky for miles

steam clouds billowing
fast as a locomotive's hot exhaust

rising in the middle of an ocean
foam-lact spreading
on the growing surface   black swells
on infant stone

2.
now her worn summits
are pale grace
and blood-green
rising from the sea

a bird swoops
into a succession
of windy valleys
down the green
and fragile spine
of land

3.
O, Bird Spirit!
quivering

whose blood screams
from the gaping vent
like a dragon's wound?
the drive stakes into it
muffling cries with cement
green stuffing ears
and bright red hands.

invisible mountain shrimp
weep

Kilauea volcano

Erratic paths run here
on black tongues of Pahoehoe
to the steaming gash.
Pink clouds signal
the collapse of edges
sliding two hundred feet
to the crust
of a rising lava lake.
Through cracks on the surface
sulphurous fumes and pink dust
burst small viscous and glowing
fountains in impossible places:

        The ceremony of magma
        ancient harmony of stone.

then out of the blue
you ask me if I'm happy
and I'm at a loss
for words to express the joy
of being in your presence

Postcard
of a Japanese Temple Garden

Here's a green picture! a garden
propped on salt and pepper shakers
on a fake marble tabletop
      curious vent: pulls me to
      green moss and stones
           real as cold air and trees

      lifting me over this edge
      to the sight of an ancient
      mountain dwelling place

There's a child here   looking for dragonflies
                            and waterlilies

now a burst of doves
startled by some dark movement
cooing fills the air
cleansing hearts of intentions
leaving space for new starts

Waimano

They came as always, all
sometimes shuffling the cold
floor trailing to the hallway
making their way boldly
to the door

feeling
nothing I'd known
yet, I freely
smiled, growing

weaker at the advance;
they came nearer, stumbling
in awkward dancing
gaits, mumbled
needs to me low,
quick grasping:
                skin
        brushed hair, clothing
                organs
me   in their asking
        Stay.

the tail of a metronome
        bent
turns the whole
mechanism Swiss-built
        deaf.
Good Mozart, flow in me.

                    Here's one:
        PARENTS: unknown
        RACE: unknown
    HEIGHT: fifty-eight inches
    WEIGHT: one hundred twenty

".......child was found at an early age, abandoned....."

Kahana

1.

sprung from jutted roots
and striking shaded mudbanks
in a volley of brown bodies
we shriek to hit the silty
river water cold
chattering in our froth and frantic
kicking to keep
the bottom muck
from sucking our feet
we race home   race out to the raft

it sinks from our weight
to a level just under
                still glowing surfaces
washing ropes over and boards
'round our ankles   lapping
'round Luka's ankles
              as he slides pole to the bottom
pushing down
leans his long weight to it
down pushing
             till the cool eddies
             chase 'round our ankles
and we are gliding
with sunken prow dipping
        past verdant Hau banks
        past a field of prickly grass
        past guava sentinels cloaked in morningglory
        past the tattered banana and a small red boat
                bobbing on a leash
          down to the wide mouth
        where surface silt glistens

Pualani's hair falls gleaming to the tips
of breasts visible in a filmy shirt
and Luka grins
pushing his pole harder
till it lodges
at the bottom
            he cannot lift it
            he clings to it
               grinning

we glide from under his feet
                    his body
arching over the surface
                    splashes
and laughing   we pitch
to the loss of
                    Pua scrambles
screaming to the center
                    we are sinking
water to my knees
I sink even deeper
                    to my waist
crawling
slipping on boards
                    to lend my weight to her's
when Luka comes slithering under
his slippery skink glowing
as we huddle
all three at the center
washed over and rubbed
by ropes   loosed
                    floating about us
                    binding us
                    trailing ends
                    on the surface
while under us
at the silty bottom
lusty Samoan crabs
begin to dance

2.

we crouch on Hau tree leaves
sparing our breath to hear
the invisible dance
of keen-whiskered mountain shrimp
in lairs   cool under
branches   and spread ourselves
on dirt   smiling hard
for wearing only each other's pleasure
beneath
tangled
slow-growing limbs
on which yellow Hau tree blossoms
                    turn to crimson

the waiting child

for the fourth grade class at Kalaheo Elementary School, Kauai

at first I was
  not used to
taking a green
tunnel into a child's heart
  but by the second
day   I began
  to suspect whose heart
it really was
the third time
I went anxious
  to meet the waiting
  child who told me of
  a dream I had
bright grinning
  at my surprise
fourth!   day
green
the tunnel   no longer
weeps the children
pull me   laughing
to an old room
wrapped in pastures
and the same dark row
of trees   cows
have been gazing at
for hours before
the arrival   we dream
                of wild ducks
              and horses
                    blood
              and water
                    pebbles
              and five

days happen
as if nothing
suddenly   real
ends.   Now
gazing
at the dark row   how!
        i dream   of bursting
                through wrappings and pastures
                        of unbroken
                                grass   frantic
                                        to find still
                                                a child there
waiting.

VOICE: 'on the dawn of the day of my discovery
                    bright containers, myself among them,
                        littered the field; our labels gone
                            dull luster of memory dimming
                        me back to dead sleep   and everything
                        growing smaller, darker, into chalk: my
                        bones'

                    I had not yet found my own humanness,
                        so I said,   "dance!
                                come dance your drooling
                    trot
                                    for me; come!
                                    I'll sing."
                            and so, I danced.

when beauty clung fast
to his neck the poet knew
the most loving act
of any lifetime ever
could be flung like rose petals

The Spring

1.
the good mid-morning air
of a green day rose
cool from her still
growing surface

a small pool fed
by the new spring

from just before dawn
of a country day

her sound
the sound
of silver
and reeds seeping

the sound of her
early wetness growing
dark and deep

the flyweight boxer
would come home drunk and be told
that I was naughty
he would lean into the crouch
solve the problem with his fists

sweet welling

in light
the awkward cattle
coming
with their thirst
to her sides

a duckling wading
and two dogs on their way
walked through her

a kitten came to sniff her
and touch

men came

and nodded
bringing their cups
to her

shining
all sweat
and tin cups

their brown skin
shining in their smiles
nodding
nodding.

continued

2.
and one of them
the first to drink

spat
himself dry

"It's bad!"
he said,
"there's salt in it!"

and the duckling
waded

through her
the kitten

didn't drink
gently
but touched her
sending

light circles
on her surface

trailing
to the center
to the sides
lapping crisply
on grass
blades
faintly

"the cattle
will grow
thin,"

they said,
"that settles it!"

"Stop it up with mud."
"Stop it up with mud."

and watching the kitten
a man
got himself up
to say,
"but then

i kinda like
the look of her

there
glowing
where she shouldn't be
maybe

but she's nice
to look at
there"

"The cattle!"
they said.

who can resist
the centering of circles?

the mad arrow
and the potter's clay
are moving parts
in a universe of motion

even the smallest
gesture of lovers
points the way

as a windshift
tells the tillerman
the way to lean

deep into the moonless
night of his dreaming

even defiance sways us
back on course

another sunset

you know,
i've only gotten
past your face
to the tide pools: patches of snow

sun's fading.
tomato soup's
warming in the dark
house we enter
            chilled from sitting
            on the seawall

I punch my son's face
lost in the ocean of time
smelling my own blood
and I am in the closet
hiding again from the blows

i'd wear you warm

i would
trace the rim
of this round
table between us

encircling you in a fiery wish to melt

and get past the cold
soup   to your face
and sauce-rimmed mouth

the roar! and sour
smell of seaweeds
sucking us
into the dead
center
of a growing
and surrounding
fire.

distant train whistle
wails in the foggy night air
you approach the bed
intentionally to give
yourself to my longheld want

"Look! I want to say
you've driven me trite!

down cobblestone sounding
cold

"are those Poplar or Maple?"
I think of
asking your face

crossing early
the wide way
to the benches

framed by unnamed trees

I think of holding
your face

then turn to find you
staring

"God, the Poplars"

and think to look
to the pale
furling undersides
of new leaves
translucent
and shivering

for the wind
comes damp on us
from the East River.

Guardrail

to the edge a frail
guardrail holding us
offering little support
as we lean out
over the pit;
the air cold
and raw on us   flayed
her skin falling in a roar
in a roar on us   sucked
down   down
to black water
and you   Stumbling!
Fool!   There's life in you!
hold on   hold on!

there is good in you
that will come through in the end
defying the odds
tenaciously holding on
to what really matters most

Love Letter

Waking, I think, "The letter's to be mailed."
It sits there on the bedstand: real. Morning
isn't. Sealed,   it's heavier than my hand.
In morning light, I can almost see
whole words through the envelope water-mark.
Last night, haste sealed it. And now aching
to tear it open, I would read it once before posting.
But then I'll burn it and nothing
would be real or said, I think. So I sit
brooding about what's real or unsaid,
said or unreal at three a.m.
at noon, the postman's
due in an hour.

when I'm not with you
I can't remember your face
but when I'm with you
I tremble in your presence
one of us must be a ghost

When Things Need Saying

her eyes
jump to the sight
of an iridescent lizard
green as sun
on the Guava branch
by the swing rope
shouting,

"don't hurt him"

then turning
gives her voice
freely sung
in meter clocked
to her breathing
to me

and when things need saying
I think

what shall I say
that will not grow small?

*I will never stop
trusting your tender mercy
o forever friend
with your soon-forgiving heart
and slyly-welcoming smile*

ipu

for Kumu Mililani Allen

dry gourd
open-neck held
high
the air is waiting
dancers enter
to fill the eye
and the plant's mouth speaks
in the hands
of another vessel
their voices intertwine
in chant
deep throated pulse
inexorably advancing
beneath a sung tale of ancient love
bodies swaying
landscape moving
all blossoming

*O fertile meadow
from exquisite loam grown wild
with the promised bloom
I see the seed of greatness
sown in your mortal beauty*

Seaside Inn - Molokai

The trump card she held
had nothing to do with me
until she played it – hard
slammed to the table
slapping thighs, shrieking
her pleasure through me
through Keawe branches
out over the water.

They shuffled chairs
to deal a new hand
and swallowed beer
chewed nuts
to break up their smiles
and whistled.

Her bulk swayed
the frail table
swayed
the company

and I thought up
reasons to love her.
She required it!
though broad straps
of her halter
were buried in flesh
and her teeth were dull
she required love
and reasons i thought.
I stood waiting
for her to win.

life is like a maze
yearning to find the exit
at each turn I make
I want to follow the light
surrender myself to grace

November's Lesson

1.
"It's a way to go," I say, "Shift fast and trip
a notch." Up. Down. Subtle, subtle;
settle to a fine focus: bastard armber.
Now, stay. "I dare you to love," I say
and make you. Sit. Careful. Petulant. Petulant
membranes slip into focus and out and into
your turning. Sit careful. Believe, I come caring. Intent
on focus, I slip, catching on grooves. Intent
on shifting, I sit, loving the hue your face
assumes. This clarity quivers me cold. November
says: This warmth is amber, bastard and barittle.
Quiver into focus, Love. These edges slip.

2.
Dark's the flood that draws
headward flown from deep
as drawn breath
                    my brawny
pump's primed so sleeping
cannot drown the paced
tides and waking
                    weeps.
The dawn's full: your face
grown deeper
                         richer
warmer than this light I taste
rising.
                    Now, now, the latches
to the doors
                    all are sprung.
Through leaves, through branches
high, higher
                    dispersing
the common, a desperate run
of sparrows stalks this morning
burnt light
                         and suns
snap in light-frames winged
burst to burst   through
                         colored air

                    settling
a moment caught tight
now slivering the air
                         lifting
loose
                    they soar from sight
roaring
                    their loss roaring.

3.
Crossing fields of fine Pahoehoe lava
blue-green flakes like scaling paint
in sunlight. Patches of rock sucked brown
Here are faults. Open. Drawn black crevices
inhaling for ages the silt of ash and pumice.
the way is a leap from edge to slipped edge.
"Leap," says salt in the wind from sea, "from flow
to flow."
                    Nothing's lost here.
Forms, memorized by lava, tell clearly
of November when light slivered earth and whole
days were fractured, spilling marrow in their rage.
A slope of agony, hardened to grooved surfaces,
can be walked. The stone furnaces
contain amber light.
                    Now, my way's the stone's
way to the shore,
                    face to the crusting salt,
to an edge where ocean slips,
                    shows a plainer
life, packed on bright sandstone.
                    Quivering.

meadow at the far
side of the stream at my feet
beckons me to cross
I yearn to give my whole being
to the open field of your mind

89

Divers

1.
3:30 p.m.
the dustpath
turns into hot sand
slopes steeply
then gently
to the water

edges out
till it surrounds
like tentacles
of hair streaming awai
from masked faces

it's a backyard
we're swimming off of.
houses here have kids
dogs, cats
lovers, enemies
and friends
inside

they've been over an hour
exploring sea-cavern
secrets to return to

      the boy has lost
      the man's fins
      and returns for days

      searching rough murky water
      for pieces of hard rubber
among black rocks and frightened fish.

may my life be pure
an expression of caring
in kindness give me
fullness of purpose and joy
waterfall spirit burst forth

2.
he gives his fear
to the water

plunges
unveiling himself
to the surge
              to the unexpected embrace billowing
sea-plant
his hair
blossoms like music
in the colorless light

only his bright
trunks belong
to earth

the rest of him dissolves
into secrets

you help me to see
that I must be my true self
for those who love me
and who wish to see me well
it is a good transaction

crossing the Kauai channel

cabin boy!
in his bed
recalls her breast
in linen billows
seeking his small mouth
his fingers
feel the prow
sluice deeper
and deeper
gulls are wheeling
about his bunk
in an open cockpit
the tillerman's setting
a true course
thinking
it doesn't count
if you don't get there

shaving my father
I leaned into the moment
aware of the crux
we had suddenly come to
in that grim hospital room

on moving from province to province

caught a moment
in the space
between places
feeling the futility of words
truth is weightless
as the wind
affecting the course
a flung stone
caught in the break
before the arrival

he was facing death
in awkward silence we sat
I was facing life
we did not know what to say
to bridge the growing distance

it's a toy mower
with bright colored wooden blades
he pushes through grass
to mow the lawn like daddy
during the separation

simple statement

you will not
make me
say it

No!
I
SHALL

say   not say

i   I

do   wanted

not   not to

love   love

you

now
that
I
have grown up.

on the lamp lit pier
we hang nets along pilings
to harvest blue crabs
a father and son embraced
by the small circle of light

Direction

It's like straight down
the white line

road map inches
finger tracing
eyes darting
from side to
blurring side

like dying insane

wailing
the way
ahead

this room
containing my mass
is part of the search

it's a rush of stars astrologers
swarm through
looking for

father speaks to son
to speak to father to tell
the truth to himself
casting bread upon water
in the vast ocean of time

Apples

"Apples!: the youth says
"Youth is apples!"

there are no further questions
no further questions
sweetness has a core.

we have both arrived
at the meadow
with perfect timing
if one of us had not arrived
the other would suffer loss

the old spring runs clear
with new water drawn from deep
sources that taste true
to quench our desert of thirst
to fill the deepest of needs

the logic of rainbows

the mist is gone now
and everything is perfectly clear
nights end
as simply as they begin
like black beads
strung on a dream
we fall back into
screaming
who holds us?
who comforts the falling?

it is its own thing
almost this and almost that
ripe Cherimoya
green globe of tropic flavors
is edible ecstasy

beautiful spirit
you've made of me a dreamer
we're both in a daze
I come as suitor to woo
to coax ecstatic assent

after the arrival

what will you do?
will you continue
to obey?

or do we never arrive?

is it the arc
we trace that matters
after all?

from Alberta

both
from Montreal
they said,

        "from Montreal
        we've come
        by bus"

along
the walk
at the canyon's
bottom

        darkness
        upset them

from Montreal
in rabbit
bundled
on a mossed
trail

        "a treacherous
        walk
        for sixteen
        dollars"

three of us
pale
from cold
and poor light
at the bottom
of a canyon

        clawed
        Birch
        upset them

how
I clambered to the rail
at trailside
looking!
white
water
white
water
the sluicing
of black
stone
towering

                    "take care
                    take care

                    the walk
                    is wet?

the viscous
air of it
grey
rising
wetness

on fallen
Birch leaves
on moss
and under the green moss!
I saw
the two
from Montreal
disturbed.

she tossed her pigtail
over her right shoulder
and looked straight ahead
striding briskly towards the glow
pure girl determination

the pathway impulse

the pathway impulse is to kneel
at shrines of fern, moss, stone, and
fall into the flash embrace
a recklessly coupled descent
into the snapping
of frail stems.

as we sought shelter
in unconditional love
we have found our way
to each other's welcome heart
as it was just meant to be

blood

the blood on the baby's bed is mine.
Red blossoms fall
fall generations through veins
are caught by her mother
a moment
held, spilled,
flows into, from us
to some strange relative's
baby's bed

a frantic mother
little boy in the bathtub
the crazy impulse
submerges them both
he understands the impulse

ritual

it is murky on H-1
and slick as grey glass
over Red Hill   i creep
pretending to be a 4 p.m. - mile-of-a-centipede's
foot

a search through cloudbanks
for the lit mountain
the burst green:

skin of the sister snake
          lava skeleton covered
with patches of Haole Koa
and Mountain Apple pale
sliding deep into the sudden
gashes of her side-wound
gulleys and valleys
          streams trail the subtle

low curve of a water
circle

the Circle

in 7th grade classrooms
lined with maps and globes
we learn how we're drinking
our own urine and snigger making
faces at each other
squirming for the bell
to let us hike the Koolau foothills
with matches in a pocket
and secrets in the other
throbbing
pocket

gripping antlers
of Koa we slide toes
                        into grooved
dirt: the steep
trail pausing to watch
                        shrinking rooftops
and a vast sea:
            the distance: expanding!

my friend
wants to keep moving to the hideout
                        ripe in place
a kind of right time for kids
to grow up   in the mountainside
                            a ritual of boys

looking for stray seeds
in this Persimmon cookie
is a one man job
that occupies the moment
with cautious chewing

darkness says, "let go"
"give up the losing battle"
yet I will choose love
and sing the sweet song of life
to enjoy the moment of you

Nanakuli

The mountain serpent's
sides are valleys
good for plunging into
from her narrow back
skidding on leaves
down streambeds
to old lava walls.

We scramble over
black boulders
looking for a place
to begin the search.
At the shore
voices of children
fall out from under
lifted stones.

Kids on the rocks are hunting crabs.

the force of the wave
propels us to the sandy shore
we jumped off the rock
into the blue-green torrent
over and over again.

the tents of summer

I.
tents grow on grass
sand, coral, lava
      pots clanging
      kids yelling
pale waves hiss on sand
tide pools
reflect the soul
on clear days
while hermit crabs
quiver at their own vision
'no worry. no worry.'
the mountain is just behind us.

II.
we must gather Keawe
for firewood
'Mesquite' they call it in Waco
in silence
our lantern
firewood
and blankets finally complete
the warm circle staring
at stones exploding in the fire
and the Milky Way takes us in suddenly
like the cloth caterpillar
at school carnivals

I do trust in love
how else can it be explained
that we have found us
guided by our every breath
all life conspires to win our cause

look down

eyes darting
into the core

        into that chambered section
        in a clock

        into the underground lake
           we're adrift on

look down

        into the flame in us
        at the center of pure

           sweeping at us from the frozen

lake

           raising a flurry of dead leaves
           sweeping fast at us
           from the lake
           'stick close!'
           run fast down cement steps
           into a tunnel

                we've become children
                  again

able to love

                a first experience.
                  an experience

    of growing strangeness
      growing strangeness

back into the core
        into the sudden bottom
        into the center
into the heart of the beloved

the waiting child

        into the mountain
        into the sulfurous vent

into the deep wounds

        at their center
        the common meaning.

black mermaid

in the deep water
　　the blue water
in the carriage house
behind the stables
in a lava lake
swimming in my soul
black mermaid
in a mirror sea
rinsing stones from her hair
in a pool of glass

　　　　of redness
　　　　so young

black mermaid in a grass field
running my soul
black mermaid in a leaf
pile stones on her eyes
her eyes are water

you're a reflection
on the skin of deep water
ineffable light
more delicate that blossoms
I can touch with spirit hands

The Matter is Time

stop pulling me

i am no longer bound by you
except as I have stored,   bound
your parts   disassembled

in the attic
my secret victim

i have already loosened
the bindings

releasing the covey
to the sun
a consequence of their explosions
blows like a chill wind
through the garden

cooling the sun
turning the pages

Manapua Man
"manapua, pe-pei-au!"
through the alleyways
balancing 5 gallon tins
from the pole on his shoulders

108

Pa Lehua: on the ridge

roots
moss and lichen
scale the crumbling path
here is a place of evergreens
of Lehua and clouds crowding us
into crevices and hairline faults
dare we plant ourselves
where plantation men might see us
from their fields?
whole mountains already swept to sea
are plowed under inside of us
darkening our breath
and our crevices are filled
with emerald voices

God of my life's core
whose name dwells under my breath
like some vital sign
of your quickening presence
you've become an old habit

the forgotten road
is now concealed in the brush
worn and overgrown
yet it once led to secret
ecstasy for the lovers

109

Dark Place

clearings ahead
thickening the path
"aaaaaaoooooooooiiii"

i've beaten the count
of running feet

in the midst of the pack
outrunning even
an imagined thirst
suns are radiating loss
gullies have lost their way
to the sea

in the event of fire
they told us not to jump.
Where the hell are they now
that the heat is on?

.........but what I mean to say is
i can't do it correctly.

your mouth
filled with words
my tongue seeks

like hot rocks
a serpent
might coil about

all salvaged from the gully

your eyes exploding
in me
shattering distant mirrors
scattering debris

smoke trailing
serpentine into the clear sky

whose life was it
i must change?

110

Time for soliloquy

needs no haste
no forethought

silent talking
to the darkness

'witness'
'witness'

new thread
has entered
the loom

when I wake to pee
she runs ahead of me
gray cat in the night
waving her tail in the air
thinking it's time for a treat

now in my despair
I find strength in your presence
and unfailing love
in my time of utter need
you provide complete safety

The Oldest Son

He always washes dishes
late at night pretending
mama's in the bedroom singing
and daddy's snoring on the couch.

But they've all fled to bed by now
through strange hallways still
clutching the snapped ends.

Desperate angels urging him
to gather them like reins
on startled horses, are weeping.

the rinsing of hands has become a ritual.

in dark storm-tossed seas
I see the glimmer of light
that shows the way home
for the wandering pilgrim
to the safety of your love

Black mirrors

gaped holes
before us are sucking
us in

black   plunging
faster   faster
the vortex slips me
into a slippery core
feet first

sucking wind after
flashes   heavy clanging memory: a grate
                                                        clang!   the grate
                                                        clang!   the grate

                                the pitch of my soul
                                is absolute   bones
                                still shiver
though fear has gone: peeled off in layers
there's no humor to be found
and I'll not amuse myself
with back-porch grief

the truth is: i am trying to understand
                        why you and i have fallen
                        into separate darknesses

birdlike memories
long hidden in the shadows
shivering in fear
are released to the new air
revealing themselves at last

Monterey Bay

cold
      granite   sand   seaweeds:
                        a conglomerate of smells
                        and bright vision
seabirds skimming
                        become a thousand spirits
                            circling the sun
            otters play
their deadly games
with shellfish
and kelp is everywhere
i tumble
looking for remnants
of the struggle
                        circling
the kelp is everywhere
in heaps of stifling coils
i leap through
groping for the shape
of this strange buried
shore

Azalea red
planted in a rock garden
meant to give comfort
ah, we control our destiny
by the small choices we make

Pot Luck

"It always seems to turn out fine!"
is echoed down the double line
of folk heaping and picking their way
to the sweets at the end of the table,

      strangers distracted by the spread on their plates
      old-timers, reaching for their favorite dishes.

Talk of folks starving never surfaces
and the Lord is praised behind His back
for everything imaginable.
In the adjacent field, mongoose wait.
Moon and mountain sing
unheeded, a song for the dying.
Tables wiped, chairs folded
scraping, rinsing and wrapping done,
they go home leaving stillness
in their wake.
In the stillness a young believer stares
past black mountains.
his song, startling the hunbry rodents,
will be forgotten.
But the pain discovered effortlessly
will guide.

a little dried leaf
dangling from spider web thread
in the gentle breeze
twirls with its own lively will
sly butterfly imposter

To a father and son

I've stumbled somehow
into your garden
full of weeds.
Here the old vine still
bears the traces of the growth
that   once graced this path
and this young shoot
of that early place
in the weathered trunk
already shows the hardiness
of the species
secure in its thicket
of dry thorns.
This is a garden of pain.
There are finer looking gardens
down the way.
But in none of them
do I find myself
asking myself,
"now, what do I really know
    of love?"

*the handsome young man
with the green Anaconda
wrapped around his body
gently kisses its small head
like that of a beloved child*

Grandmother

did I once see a kimono'd woman
go up the wooden steps?

is she cutting Chrysanthemums
in her room
her warm face entering the white blossom?

sudden Kona storm
I smell rain in the grey sky
winds of doubt rush
I yearn to be unwound
to back before creation

Makaha

when auntie picks leaves
from the grass
she sings
her smile like hibiscus
blooms in sunlight
her eyes follow the wind
to find him
whose voice she hears

whispering "love one another"
she holds each speckled Croton
leaf with thumb and forefinger
feeling the cold veins like ribs

we've been cast into
a dreamlike poetry realm
where surface is truth
and everything discovered
reveals more than just itself

when I crash and burn
doves return empty-handed
to the sinking ark
of our human condition
it's a fellowship of pain

Vine

i feel as though pulled
from fertile ground at birth

and filled with living water

no mere refreshment
but more than change itself
reveals an unchanging love

flowing, undiminished,
through all things created
from root to branch to fruit

fragrance of the feast
evokes treasured memories
of precious ones gone
we hold that lingering ache
and reach out to each other

let me use these clouds
to teach you how I love you
see how they reflect
fiery colors of the sun?
like my heart in your presence

Gasping

My inmost chambers
wrapped by tentacles;
for shame, I gasp
at breath I've squandered
on things I wouldn't set
my soul upon at last

were that choice
also mine.

a nick draws dark blood
unexpectedly venous
pupils dilated
seeing shapes beyond the veil
reconciliation time

beautiful spirit
I'm sorry for making you
angry yesterday
there's no redemption for me
but to be put in my place

Trust

Brother of my heart,
willfully hurt
by my hand
were this my own blood
could I feel less
the wound suffered?

Forgiveness does not regain
what, once spilled, flows
to the anonymous sea.

I shall not question
the rain.

pair of mourning doves
motionless in Zen garden
blending into rock
the eyes of tranquility
see into my racing heart

all we have is now
shall we squander the moment
or make it amount
to some eternal value
confess our love one more time

Watching Him Die

I felt the release of
        the burst seam
        the snapped reins like rifle shot aimed at distant
        hills.

The child
bearer of sins
is cast into the arms
of those herded into
the grim
hold.

And mountains float in space
while the held child
is comforted.

wounds have clotting times
ranging from a few seconds
to infinity.

Azalea dream
surrounds the heart with beauty
at the end of sleep
a profusion of blossoms
to adorn the waking soul

A Divine Presence Among Us

anemones washed
like butterfly petals
sing brighter than stones
in the sky

O, cares
loosed to the air;
your caress is the wind
enfolding my skin.

Held still,
I gaze at love;

still bound by thy presence
I am found.

looking at the moon
I yearn to see my best self
then I see the sun
reflected back to my life
and the light is forgiveness

begging for money
on Grand Avenue she is
someone's grandmother
peering straight into my soul
as I open my wallet

This business

of sloughing the old
skin is serious business
for old serpents
and their kin.

what can I not say
that impels me to take notes
at 2 a.m. on my phone
to capture the dragonflies
of splattered blood from the bomb?

the pain in your eyes
glows amber as you choose words
to reveal hard truths
releasing them to the air
between us inviting care

I keep returning
to that beachfront house in dreams
now to prepare it
for a really big event
my daughter is here to help

gardener at the shore

for Duane Allen

the sound of waves crashing on a reef
threatens to crush
his stem
and when he's had enough
of other people's
gardens
he goes home
to his own

the plucked string resounds
finite wave decays in time
the voice of truth wails
impotent consolation
for the burning of children

living is messy
we end up with dirty feet
simply showing up
reluctant protagonists
fighting the retrograde wish

there will come a time
when yearnings are realized
and reality
will extend beyond the realm
of all conceivable good

On Puuloa heading north

At the roadside
    pieces of tissue
    caught in drying koa
    like petals   stiff
    with the phlegm of strangers
    flutter
    at 30 mph: morningglory
    blossoming
    in a rear-view mirror
And ahead on a hillside
tired army nurses
trail gauze
in their caring
scurrying down corridors
wheeling bouquets
before them
silently
       to that space
in the fold
of an amputee's sleeve
where villagers
and whole villages
have already
gone
yesterday
i sat hours
looking for dragonflies
in a huge Monet.

in this tsunami
of love we've been swept away
to a high valley
of bamboo groves surrounding
the meadow we can call home

Parting of the loaf

round as warm stones
held
a simple pressing on softness
of thumbs over and fingers
hollowing the bottom
a twisting of wrists
between us gently
fraying
smooth crust
in blessing
the lifting of fingertips
under
rifting crust and insides
rising of heat
moist as the sight
of a single loaf's breaking
portions
uneven but sufficient
tell each of holding
parts of others
of giving in the parting
as when yeast in us
says,
      "be more"
   O, once
    we held the sun
    in smaller hands
    than these.

it's a happy place
this lily pad we've come to
on our journey home
so many hops to get here
only a few more to go

127

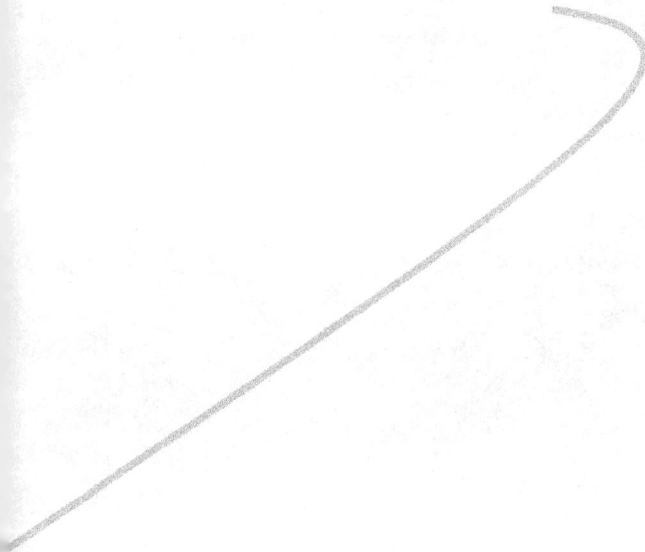

LOVE TANKAS

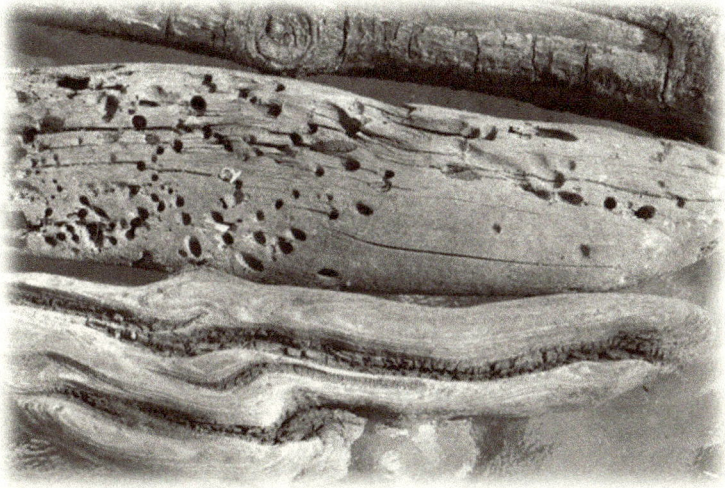

LOVE TANKAS

129

I'm in a bright meadow
when in my heart's eye you stand
tall and evergreen
beauty to last a lifetime
of remembering this love

the pen is a sign
of enduring truth and troth
even were it to be lost
the tale of souls intertwined
is writ indelibly bold

I am the Poet
who once loved your near double
in another time
complicating the present
with echoes of devotion

you were my lover
in another perfect life
I have not yet mourned
that death on that sad island
some losses remain unsaid

you've plucked chords in me
to forgotten songs long-stilled
to songs unwritten
whose meanings are in the wind
whose tunes live in our bodies

I keep replaying
in my mind the accident
over and over
again and again filling
my heart with such emptiness

does my pure love count
for currency in this game?
have I no credit
to affect the final score
am I now irrelevant?

we must discover
why the universe has sent
this humble servant
into your earthly service
undoubtedly to do good

every time I see you
you just take my breath away
your mortal presence
defies mere reality
and I am delusional

all is unspoken
the melody goes unheard
but ancient meanings
bind the poet and the boy who stand
in totally different nows

in you I have found
someone I thought I had lost
I keep finding you
in unexpected places
in unsuspecting people

when beauty clung fast
to his neck the poet knew
the most loving act
of any lifetime ever
could be flung like rose petals

there is good in you
that will come through in the end
defying the odds
tenaciously holding on
to what really matters most

I will never stop
trusting your tender mercy
o forever friend
with your soon-forgiving heart
and slyly-welcoming smile

O fertile meadow
from exquisite loam grown wild
with the promised bloom
I see the seed of greatness
sown in your mortal beauty

133

meadow at the far
side of the stream at my feet
beckons me to cross
I yearn to give my whole being
to the open field of your mind

I am now reduced
to yearning to kiss your feet
my lips drawn downwards
by the force of this desire
to taste your hidden shyness

you help me to see
that I must be my true self
for those who love me
and who wish to see me well
it is a good transaction

the old spring runs clear
with new water drawn from deep
sources that taste true
to quench your desert of thirst
to fill your deepest of needs

we have both arrived
at the meadow
with perfect timing
if one of us had not arrived
the other would suffer loss

as we sought shelter
in unconditional love
we have found our way
to each other's welcome heart
as it was chosen to be

darkness says, "let go
give up the losing battle"
yet I will choose love
and sing the sweet song of life
to enjoy the moment of you

I do trust in love
how else can it be explained
that we have found us
guided by our every breath
all life conspires to win our cause

you're a reflection
on the skin of deep water
ineffable light
more delicate than blossoms
I can touch with spirit hands

this year marks the birth
of love that could not be kept
contained in one heart
but like a wild fire subsumes
us both in its ecstasy

may we dedicate
this freshly minted annum
to the learning of love
that defies all boundaries
and leads us to bliss unknown

now in my despair
I find strength in your caring
and unfailing peace
in my favorite meadow
the safest haven on earth

in dark storm-tossed seas
I see the glimmer of light
that shows the way home
for the wandering pilgrim
to the safety of your love

I would hold you long
after our passion has spent
itself to ashes
gently cradling your beauty
in worshipful arms and awe

when you said to write
you did not know what fountains
would burst forth to give
voice and form to such passion
this universe could not hide

in the tsunami
of our love all measurements
have lost their meanings
there is only the vastness
of what was meant to become

inimitable
style in life and love
you've broken the mold
and allowed the molten gold
to spill out into new space

then out of the blue
you ask me if I'm happy
and I'm at a loss
for words to express the joy
of being in your presence

I would play you now
like a well-tuned instrument
and cause you to hum
with utter satisfaction
content to glow in the dark

I would play you loud
like a shiny instrument
I would play you soft
like a finely polished curve
I would make you hum for joy

I will gently guide
you over that fearful edge
into utter ecstasy
give yourself to the pleasure
freely offered, freely take

we have danced this dance
before in dream encounters
spontaneously
our spirits have rehearsals
when we aren't even watching

I accept torment
is the price that must be paid
to be in your world
within soft touching distance
close enough to feel your heat

beloved I hurt
just thinking of you homeless
and alone those nights
I could have held you tightly
in my warm sheltering arms

all history points
to the moment when your arched
bow of a taut back
becomes the arrow's release
like stars bursting in night sky

by naming a thing
we can put distance between
us and this demon
this destroyer of my peace
this shatterer of the calm

there's no denying
that we've been placed together
for some great purpose
it is our task to find out
what it is and achieve it

we've been cast into
a dreamlike poetic realm
where surface is truth
and everything discovered
reveals more than just itself

now how can it be
that I have fallen deeper
into love with thee?
I was already too deep
to exhale without aching

o, my love, true light
of my life, you are sunshine
to my morning heart
your displeasure is my hell
I only seek your sly smile

I actually fear
that even these gifts of verse
might ignite your ire
and prompt you to banish me
from the kingdom of your smile

let me use these clouds
to teach you how I love you
see how they reflect
fiery colors of the sun?
like my heart in your presence

what more can be said
than I love you, I love you
I love you my love
what more do you need to hear?
there is only this to say

we both have always
known that this was meant to be.
inevitable
from the start the yearned for goal
was always within our reach

after a charmed night
I am mesmerized and dazed
by the truth of you
revealed by your luscious lips
between hits of corn cob pipe

I am bedazzled
by the dense complexity
of your wondrous being
my heart does worship you whole
your body is my temple

this is my joyful hell
to yearn to touch your body
yet not be allowed
into that garden of bliss
tormented by the mere thought

love, put me out of
this perpetual agony
grant release I pray
to this prisoner of want
with a simple opening

your body drives me
nuts, your raised thigh is a highway
to your fair meadow
where this pilgrim imagines
unspeakably wild pleasures

keeper of my heart
you are gentle and caring
I know I am safe
in your strong and loving hands
as you guide us on this path

you asked for a bro
and got a poet instead
who can be a bro
but also so much much more
like an unexpected gift

after a lifetime
of frantic searching I've found
the love of my life
in you my perfect lover
we've waited for this moment

if infinity
dawns in us everyday
why is it your name
I call out in the morning
and whisper at end of day?

I cherish your mind
far more than I could ever
cherish your body
for the union of ideas
fits more perfectly than flesh

my wounded spirit
still remembers how to pray
for you my beloved
I pray that you will find her
the mother of your children

the poet in love
soothes the fluttering heartbeat
of the beloved
with earnest words and gestures
to protect the budding bloom

but how can it be?!
that I have found you my love
master of my soul
standing tall in the sunshine
like a miracle waiting

there will come a time
when yearnings are delivered
and reality
will expand beyond the realm
of all conceivable good

when I'm not with you
I can't remember your face
but when I'm with you
I tremble in your presence
one of us must be a ghost

I do trust in love
how else can it be explained
that we have found us
guided by our every breath
life conspires to win our cause

A Lyric Poem

beloved I would feel the length
of your fingers and stretch their span
to feel the tautness in your thumb
and the softness of your palm.
I would kiss the tips of your fingers

just to do so.
I would run my finger down each ridge of
your hand. And fold my interlocking
fingers with yours to share their warmth
to feel our souls blending

you're my soul partner
in the most primitive dance
you give and I take
you push and I pull till you
slip out of reality
into pure satisfaction

mulberries

four years after my stroke
and sometime before my final breath
I eat my very first mulberry
delighting in the firstness
of the experience
intrigued by the sight
of subtle royal hues
discrete clusters of little globes
like tiny heads
each cluster a thing
bloomed, evolved and transformed
in the fruiting process
ripened in place
in sun and shade
hand-picked by the young farmer
who searches among the leaves and branches
fingers gently lifting each found treasure
mulberries for silkworms
grow in Phnom Penh
where heads of infants were once bashed
against tree trunks
their sticky juice seeping down to roots
air filled with wailing
to contaminate the wind
I tremble at the thought of my first taste
of this fruit

Elegy for Alex

The warehouse is empty
not a grain of wheat is left
just a breath in the shadow
the iridescent boy is still catching
dragonflies in a huge Monet

ACKNOWLEDGEMENTS

I am indebted to my editor, ROBT O'SULLIVAN SCHLEITH, who has been a true believer in the worth of these poems and staunch advocate for their publication. It was with utter confidence that I entrusted them to his caring and expert hands. Thank you, Robt.

Some of the poems and tankas in this collection appeared in the following publications:

Magee Park Poets
Poetry Northwest
Cimarron Review
Hawaii Review
Poetry Hawaii
San Diego Poetry Annual

CREDITS

COVER AND INSIDE TITLE PAGE: *Makaha Valley*
illustration by RILEY PRATO
based on a watercolor by THOMAS LLOYD RAMSIÈR

INTERIOR ART:
photographs by the author

PHOTOGRAPHS OF THE AUTHOR:
Cover portrait by BARBARA TAKAHARA
Interior portrait by TAYLOR LARISON

AFTERWORD

It was publisher BILL HARDING who suggested the structure for the book, beginning with current work and "floating backwards" to the early work. He intuitively knew that such a flow would organically echo the essential theme of the book, which is the discovery of the waiting child in us.

Thus, the final section, entitled *The Waiting Child*, was the first written. That book length section was completed in fulfillment of a Bachelor of Arts program for Antioch University, nearly 40 years ago. The next section written was *Embrace of the Living God*, which recounts two decades of spiritual rebirth and growth. During that phase of my life, I married, we had two children, and I worked in Social Services and as a Probation Officer while also serving as a Southern Baptist Deacon, Presbyterian Ruling Elder and Salvation Army Elder and Homeless Services Director. I also volunteered as a community activist, presiding over several non-profit boards and directing an international young artists competition for violinists and pianists, burning out every couple of years, while taking medication for hypertension. Unsurprisingly, this led to a cerebral hemorrhage/stroke in 2014, at age 72. Life since then has been post-stroke recovery.

The tankas were the result of a conscious effort to use poetry writing as a self-healing exercise for my damaged brain. The brain activities required to compose poems are precisely appropriate to help the brain repair itself. I also used the opportunity as a poet to explore my own Japanese heritage by focusing on and learning to master the ancient Japanese Tanka form. My initial collection of Tanka was entitled *From the Crucible*, which depicted my journey through disorientation, re-assemblage of self, despair and obsessive suicidality. Having already experienced a spiritual re-birth, I suddenly found myself going through a mental/emotional re-birth; struggling to rediscover my self.

Most of the *Love Tankas* were written in a delusional state during my recovery from a brain hemorrhage; which means I was stroked and smitten. I was looking for up, and found it in surprising places and people. It was an ecstatic experience.

Then, as I continued adapting daily to my new reality, I was unexpectedly given a new name. As we recently participated in a Hindu wedding ceremony for our daughter, the Swami asked for my name, which he then translated to: Mohan. When corrected by the family, he said, "Mohan is fine."

After the ceremony, he told me that because of my Karma, Krishna has given me the name "Mohan." I have since been told by Hindu family members that "Mohan" is another name of God. Thus the section of current poems which begins the book is called, *Mohan's Song*.

ABOUT THE POET

MEL TAKAHARA was born in the
Territory of Hawaii 20 days
prior to the attack on Pearl
Harbor. His ancestry includes
Japanese, Korean, Chinese,
Hawaiian and Portuguese,
reflecting that Hawaii is a true
"melting pot" of races and
cultures. He received a public
school education in the
territory and state's English
Standard School System.
graduating in 1960 a year after
Hawaii became the 50th state.

As a young teen, he was mesmerized by *A Child's Garden of Verse* by Robert Louis Stevenson. He began writing his own poems in middle school. when he attended Robert Louis Stevenson Intermediate School.

At the University of Hawaii, Mel was mentored by poet and Yeats scholar JOHN UNTERECKER, author of *Voyager: Biography of Hart Crane*, and *A Reader's Guide to William Butler Yeats*, who had been chair of the graduate department of Columbia University. Under the guidance of Dr. Unterecker, Mel earned a B.A. in Creative Writing from Antioch University.

In 1970, Mel received the Ernest Hemingway award, which was established by Hemingway's sister. For several years, he served as a Master Poet Trainer with the Hawaii State Foundation on Culture and the Arts, conducting workshops in schools on all islands throughout the state of Hawaii.

Mel's poems have appeared in *Magee Park Poets, Poetry Northwest, Cimarron Review, World Poet (published in India), Hawaii Review, Kapa, San Diego Poetry Annual* and *Poetry Hawaii, a contemporary anthology*. His one act play, *Syndrome* was produced by US Army Special Services at Fort Monmouth, New Jersey, while Mel served as an Army medic in the early '60s.

For two decades in Hawaii, Mel worked as a non-profit social services administrator for poverty programs for children and youth. In San Diego, he served as a county Probation Officer until his retirement in 2005. He then also worked at the Escondido Salvation Army and served as the system developer for the North County Homeless Shelter system. For his work with The Salvation Army, he was recipient of the 2007 Gandhi award for Faith Leader from the Tariq Khamisa Foundation.